BROCKHAMPTON PRESS

Picture Reference book of the

ANCIENT ROMANS

General Editor: Boswell Taylor
Consultant Historian: John D. Bareham, BA
Illustrator: John Pittaway
Further research by Antony Kamm, MA

CONTENTS

ROMANS TOLD A STORY that Rhea Silva, a daughter of the king of the Latins and a descendant of the Trojan hero Aeneas, had by Mars, the god of war, twin sons, Romulus and Remus. The twins were ordered to be drowned, but they were saved, and were suckled by a she-wolf. When they grew up, they decided to establish a new city on the banks of the river Tiber, and on the borders of the neighbouring Etruscans. While they were planning the boundaries, they had an argument, during which Romulus killed his brother. The city which still bears his name was founded on 21st April 753 BC. The Roman Empire which grew from its small beginnings, and which at one time stretched from Britain to North Africa, and from Spain to Arabia, lasted until AD 476, when the last Roman emperor was deposed, though the eastern half still survived in parts until the capture of Constantinople by the Turks in 1453. Though the Romans were fine soldiers, loyal and dedicated to order and justice, they could also be cruel and unfeeling. However they gave to the world many things which we use today, including our calendar. Our alphabet comes from the Romans, as well as about one-third of the words in the English language.

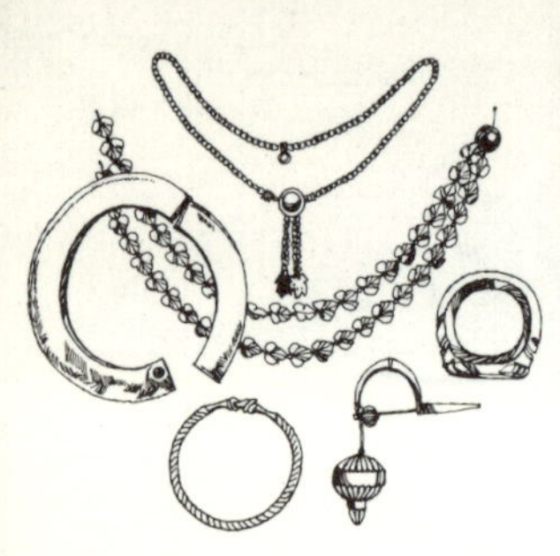

jewellery

Costume

wedding scene

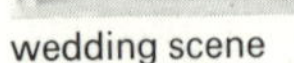

priest with fold of *toga* covering his head during religious ceremony

orator wearing *toga,* the Roman's chief outdoor garment. Underneath is the *tunica,* a short-sleeved shirt

a mother with her son and daughter; 4th century portrait in gold leaf on glass

dancing girls

bronze statue of boy in striped garment

hairstyles

marble statue of scholar with bundle of book rolls

Indoors,men and women wore a simple tunic, reaching just below the knees, The white woollen toga was worn on formal occasions and out of doors. Semi-circular in shape, the toga was about 18 feet long, and 7 feet deep at the widest part. It was draped over the left shoulder and then folded round the body. The togas of higher priests and magistrates, and of free-born youths and girls, had a purple stripe along the edge.

The Roman soldier

y-equipped legionary on the march

auxiliary cavalryman

aquilifer, the standard-bearer of a legion

slinger, whose ammunition was lead bullets or round stones

long sword or *spatha* and sword or *gladius*

building siege platforms with logs; legionaries in the background

centurions

legionaries

The legionary carried a sword (*gladius*) and javelin (*pilum*). Round his neck he wore a scarf (*focale*) to prevent the armour chafing his skin. Under the metal armour he wore a woollen knee-length tunic and, in winter, tight-fitting leather trousers (*bracae*). Each soldier carried a saw, basket, pickaxe, thong of leather, hook, and three days' rations.

Centurions wore distinctive uniforms with pleated kilts and fur-lined boots. They carried a stout vine staff as a symbol of rank.

A Roman soldier was likely to serve for twenty years or more. His training was long and hard, and he had to be able to march 20 miles in a day. The punishments for failing his duty were severe. When he was not fighting, he would be employed on building operations. His pay was small, and out of it he had to buy his bedding, clothing, boots and food. On active service he would not often have a chance to eat meat.

legionary helmet (*galea*) of bronze with iron skull-cap inside, and probably leather or cloth lining

The Roman legion

surgeon bandages auxiliary at field dressing station

The legion's standard was carried by the **AQUILIFER** who ranked just below a centurion.

IMAGINIFER
carried a standard containing medallions with portraits of reigning or deified emperors.

A legion had about 120 horsemen used mainly as orderlies and despatch riders.

Special duty men attached to a legion included paymasters, clerks, trumpeters, orderlies, builders, surveyors, engineers, catapult makers, arrow makers, soothsayers, doctors, medical orderlies.

Roman eagle from Trajan's Column, Rome

LEGATUS
After the time of Julius Caesar, the commander of the legion and auxiliaries attached to it. A professional politician, he was normally kept in his command for 3-4 years, after which he might become a provincial governor.

TRIBUNUS LATICLAVIUS
Senior Tribune
A young man serving for 2-3 years before entering the Senate.

FIVE TRIBUNES
Likely to have been local government administrators. Employed mainly as staff officers, but commanded detachments in action. Might later command auxiliary units or become civil servants.

PRAEFECTUS CASTRORUM
Camp Prefect
Senior professional soldier in the legion, usually with at least 30 years' service. Responsible for training, organisation and equipment.

A legion contained 10 cohorts. Each cohort was divided up into 6 centuries of 60-80 men

A CENTURY

CENTURION
The commander of a century. The senior centurion in the legion commanded the first century and was called CENTURIO PRIMUS PILUS.

OPTIO
Second-in-command of a century.

SIGNIFER
Standard bearer. He also looked after the century's savings bank.

TESSERARIUS
Looked after small pickets and fatigue parties.

LEGIONARIES
All Roman citizens. 8 men shared a tent and a mule to carry their gear.

roof tile showing wild bo emblem of the Twentieth Legio

AUXILIA
Light armed troops. Non-Roman inhabitants of the Empire, commanded by Roman officers.

ALAE (wings) of cavalry divided into **TURMAE** (squadrons)

COHORTS of Infantry divided into **CENTURIES**

COHORTS of Mounted Infantry

cutting corn to feed army

calthrop, thrown on the ground to hinder cavalry

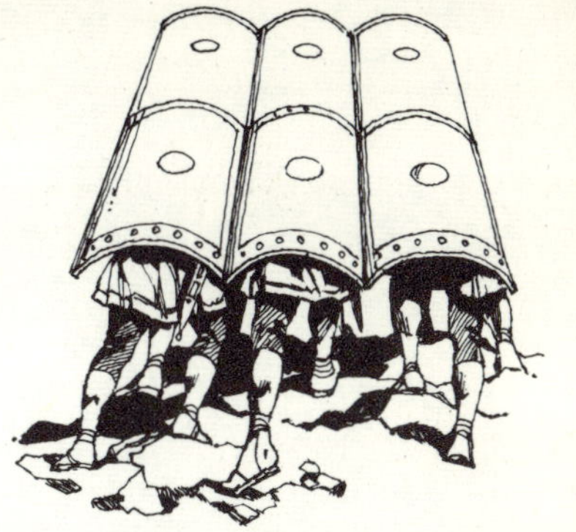

testudo of interlocking shields

At war

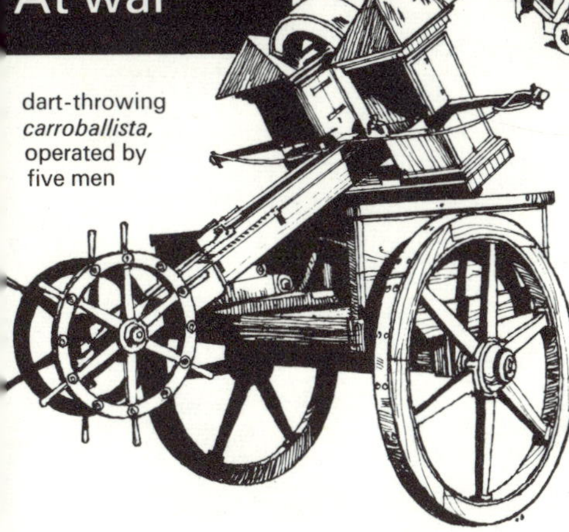

dart-throwing *carroballista,* operated by five men

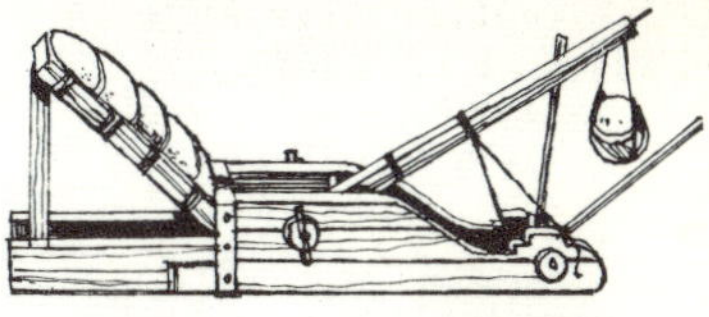

battering-ram

large catapult (*onager*) for hurling boulders

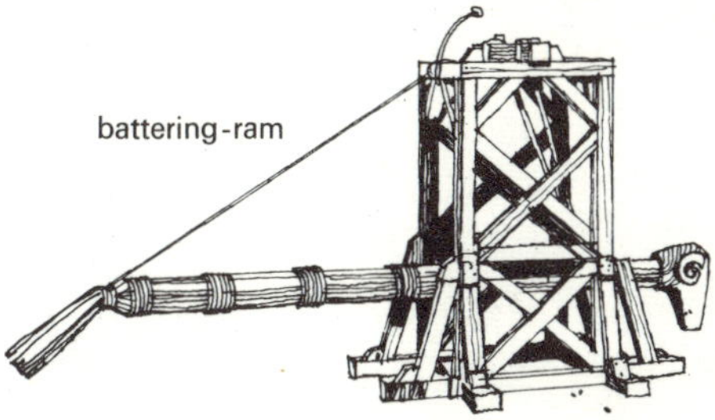

battering-ram

sarcophagus showing battle scene, with Romans fighting trouser-clad barbarians (probably Germanic) ; note the Roman commander top centre and the *signifer* in chain mail cuirass on the right

mobile assault tower with drawbridge carries soldiers on to walls of besieged cities

After each day's march, an army built a fortified camp. Soldiers were drilled to act in unison. When they attacked a walled town they protected themselves by putting their shields together over their heads like the shell of a tortoise, or *testudo*. Clever engineers, the Romans built weapons to hurl stones, and towers from which to attack walls. In battle the lines of legionaries first hurled their javelins and then closed in to fight with swords.

bringing in prisoners

The triumph

statues of Victoria, goddess of victory, were erected throughout the Roman Empire

Arch of Titus in Rome, commemorating the Jewish War of 66-70 AD

wounded Gaul

Emperor Marcus Aurelius enters Rome in triumph

execution of rebels

A victorious general could be rewarded by the Senate with a Triumph, which included a procession in which he paraded not only his army, but also his prisoners and spoils of war. It was a day of festival, and the procession would wind through the streets and up to the Temple of Jupiter on the Capitol Hill, the most sacred place in the city. There sacrifices would be held to celebrate the event.

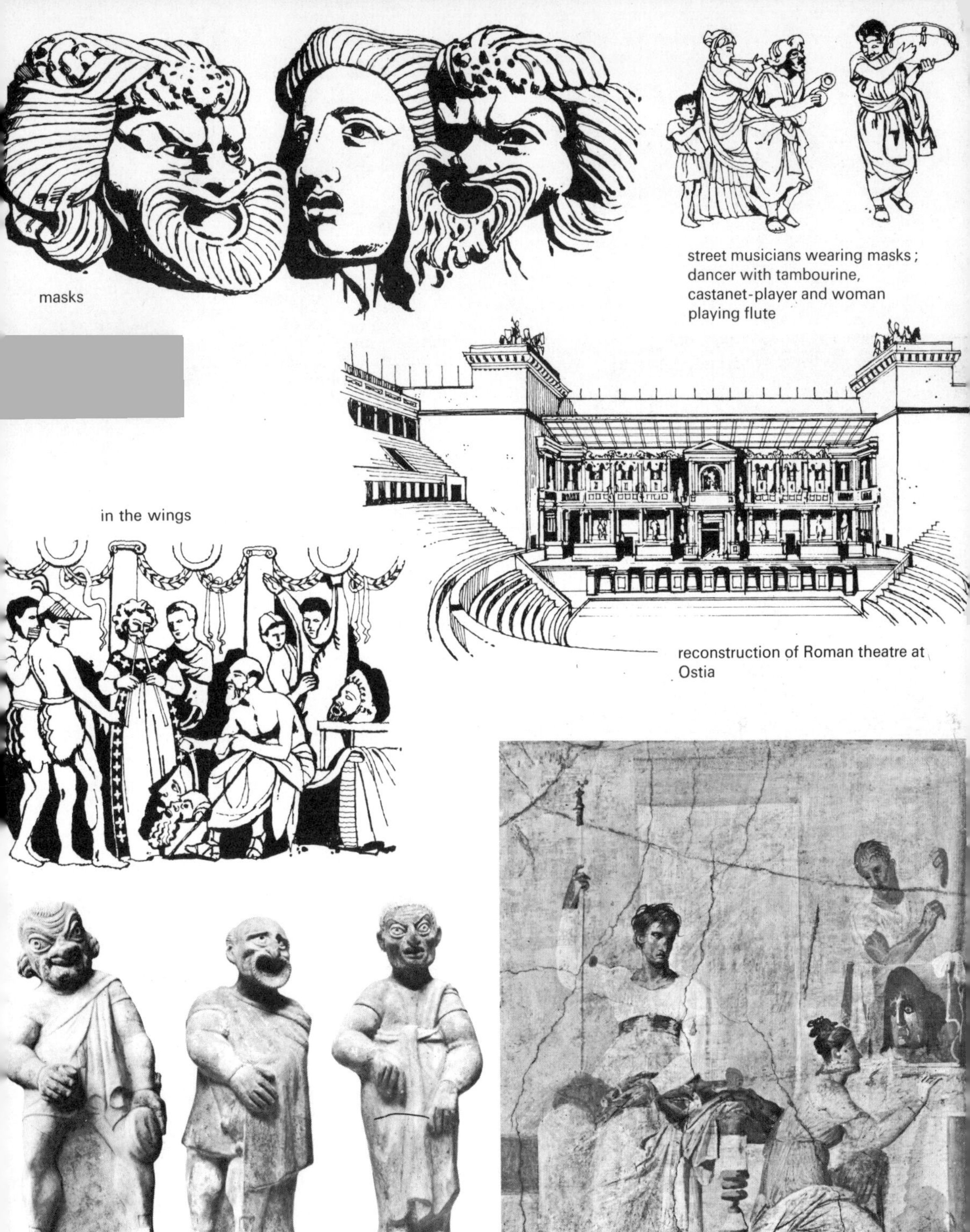

masks

street musicians wearing masks; dancer with tambourine, castanet-player and woman playing flute

in the wings

reconstruction of Roman theatre at Ostia

terracotta statuettes of actors

stage painting showing tragic king, and girl looking at mask of horror

In early Roman times, plays were performed on wooden stages by travelling players. The Romans copied their theatres and their early plays from the Greeks. The better and most influential of the surviving plays written by Romans were comedies. The actors wore masks, and were slaves or freedmen. Each seat was numbered, and tickets of bone or ivory were issued. A huge awning could be drawn over the theatre in bad weather.

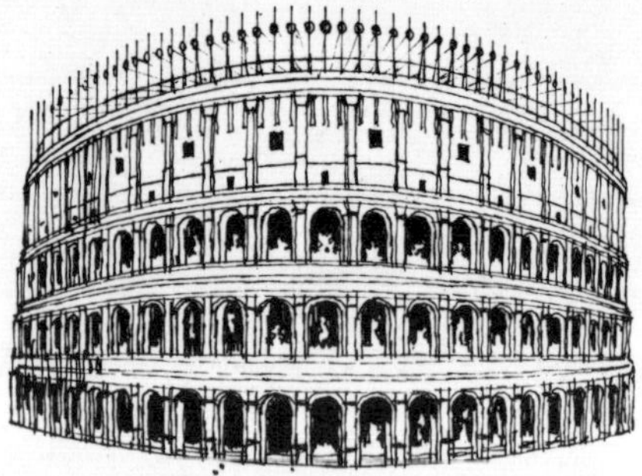

The Colosseum, amphitheatre in Rome, could hold 50,000 spectators

secutor (with sword and shield) fighting retiarius (with net and trident)

Sports and amusements

interior of the Colosseum, showing chambers beneath the arena where the wild animals were kept

gladiator wearing traditional Samnite armour

women playing knuckle-bones

gladiator fights lion and lioness
the box on the left is that of the patron of the games, and on the rack in the centre are seven eggs, one of which was removed after each event

So much work was done by slaves that free Romans had much leisure time. They went to the public baths to meet and talk, or to do gymnastics or wrestling. Public entertainment was violent and horrible. Even chariot races were dangerous to charioteers and horses. The contestants raced round the stadium with a sharp turn at each end round the narrow central barrier. Originally the death of slaves in single combat had a religious meaning, but later

quadriga, large chariot with four horses

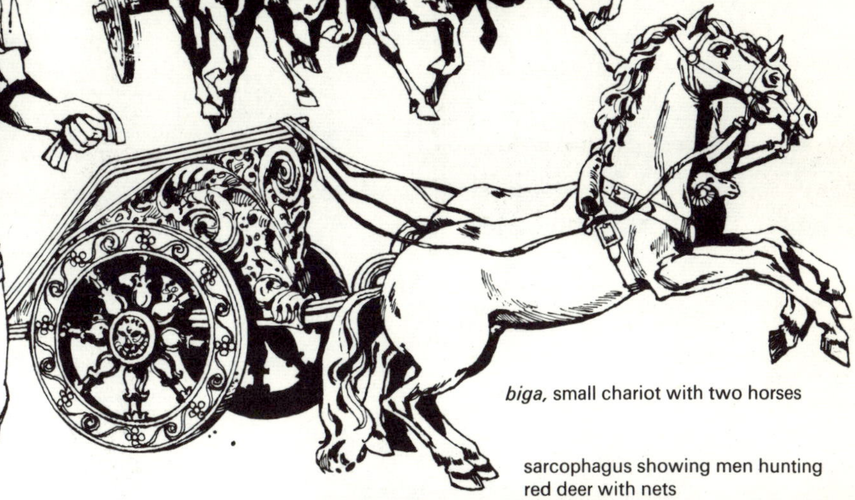

biga, small chariot with two horses

victorious charioteer with palm branch

wrestling

sarcophagus showing men hunting red deer with nets

mosaic showing gladiators in combat

hunters carrying slain boar

the slaughter of men and animals in the sand-strewn arenas was regarded entirely as entertainment. Slaves, condemned criminals and prisoners of war were trained as gladiators, knowing that in the end they would die. In 73 BC a band of gladiators under Spartacus mutinied, and collected a large army. It was two years before they were defeated. As a punishment thousands of slaves were crucified alongside the main road from Rome to Capua.

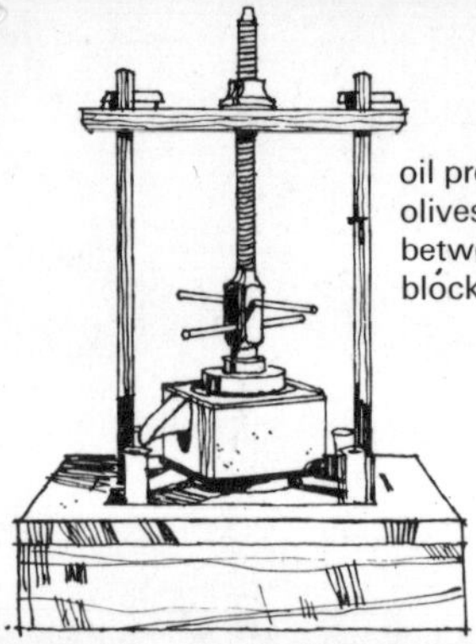

oil press;
olives were crushed between stone block and base

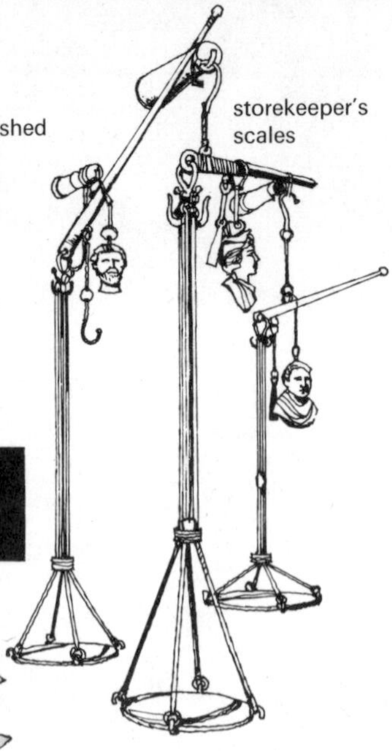

storekeeper's scales

greengrocer selling cabbage, kale, garlic, leeks and onions

Towns and trade

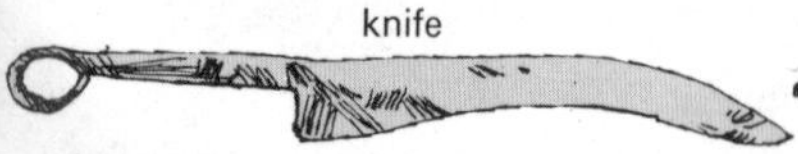

knife

cleaver

meat hook

accounts on wax tablets

thermopolium (tavern) where hot wine was served, in Pompeii's main shopping street.
Notices and announcements were often painted on walls, and the central one here indicates a shop selling oil

Merchants and traders, those who supplied the shops with goods as well as the shop-keepers themselves, were not highly regarded in Roman times, though they were much needed. Each town had its craftsmen and shops.

From different parts of Italy came particular commodities —woollens and carpets from Etruria, Patavium and Verona; red pottery from Arretium; iron from Comum; coarse clothing from Linguria. Many products were imported in

sestertius, c 54 BC, showing Nero

bronze treble sestertius with head of Septimius Severus

bronze as, c late 3rd century BC, showing two-headed god Janus

silver denarius, c 44 BC, showing Julius Caesar and Venus Victrix

pharmacies sold anything from herbs to groceries

cobbler

marble gates to a town house; the building behind has a sun porch (centre)

flour mill worked by a horse

butcher's shop

large quantities from abroad, and particularly wheat from Africa, Egypt and Sicily. Poverty was rife, and at one time corn was given away free to Roman citizens. The earliest Roman coin was the bronze *as*, introduced shortly after 300 BC. Later came two silver coins, the *sestertius* (worth four asses), and the *denarius* (16 asses). Coins bore different devices, and Julius Caesar started the great tradition of coins depicting the head of the reigning ruler.

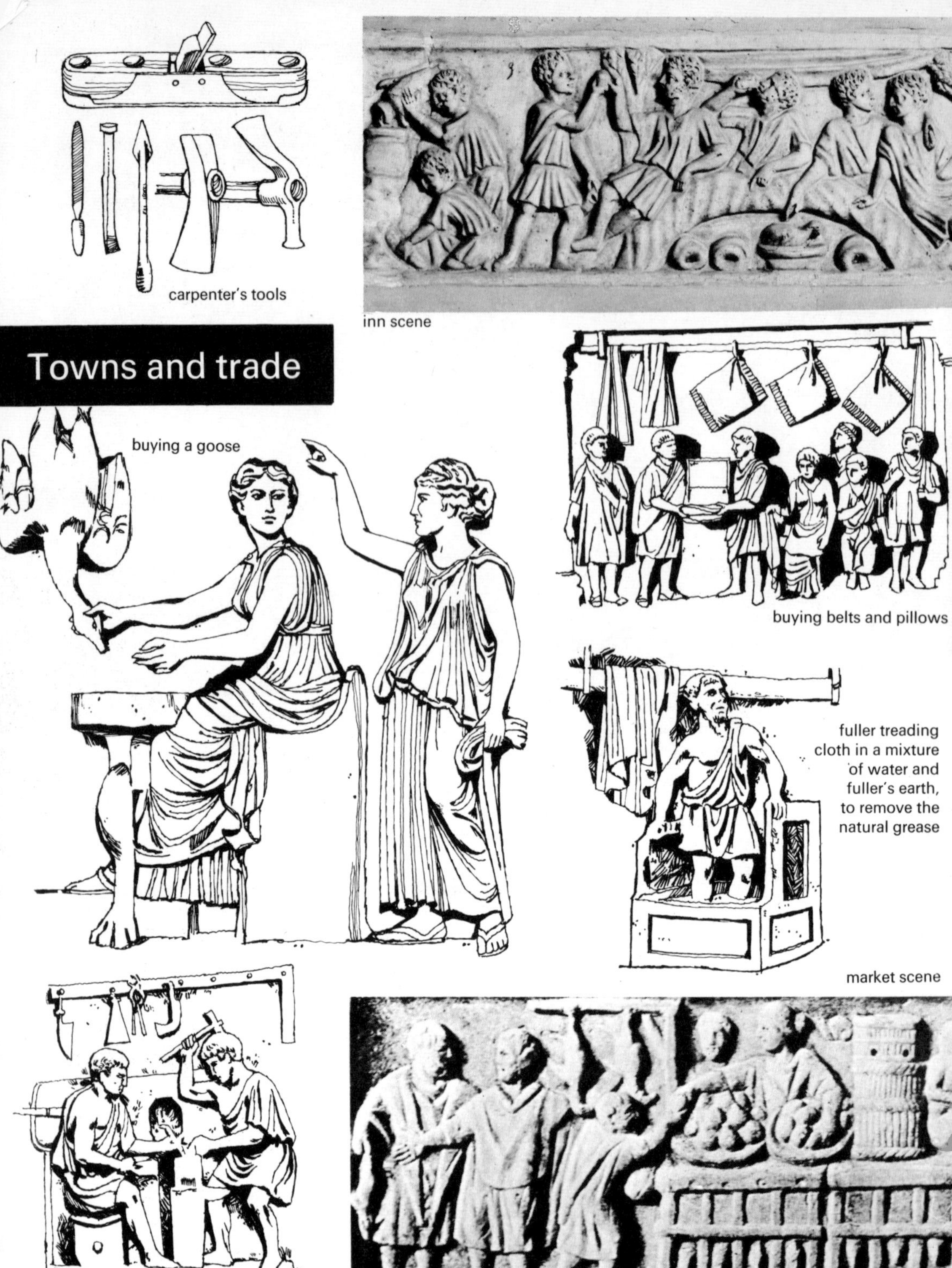
carpenter's tools

inn scene

Towns and trade

buying a goose

buying belts and pillows

fuller treading cloth in a mixture of water and fuller's earth, to remove the natural grease

market scene

cutler's workshop; one man works bellows while another hammers on an anvil

Roman towns were laid out to a set pattern, like the army camps, with four gates from which two main roads crossed each other at right-angles at the centre of the town. Around the central forum, originally also the market-place, were the important buildings of the town, the law court, the meeting place for the governing body, and the public baths. In the market-place, traders of the same kinds of goods tended to keep their shops or stalls

copper coin showing Trajan and Forum

potin (base-silver) coin of Sabina Augusta, wife of Hadrian

copper coin of 118 AD showing Hadrian and Britannia

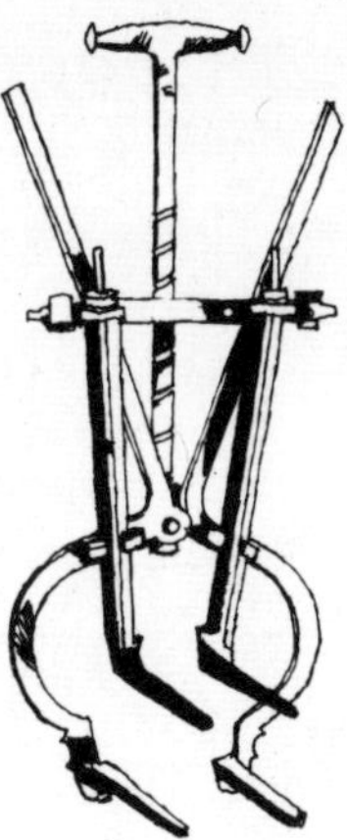

medical instrument

North Gate of Trier, city of Gaul

walnuts and bread, baked nearly 2,000 years ago, from Pompeii

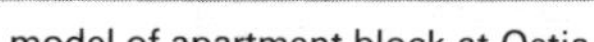

model of apartment block at Ostia

peasants paying rent in cash

humpbacked beggar

together. There would be temples, and often a theatre and a library. Many town-dwellers lived in blocks of flats, which were allowed to be up to 65 feet high. Some badly-built blocks crashed to the ground. Each province of the empire was looked after by a governor, who was responsible for keeping order, administering justice and collecting taxes. Some provincial towns were enlarged from existing towns. Others were built to house retired soldiers.

Country life

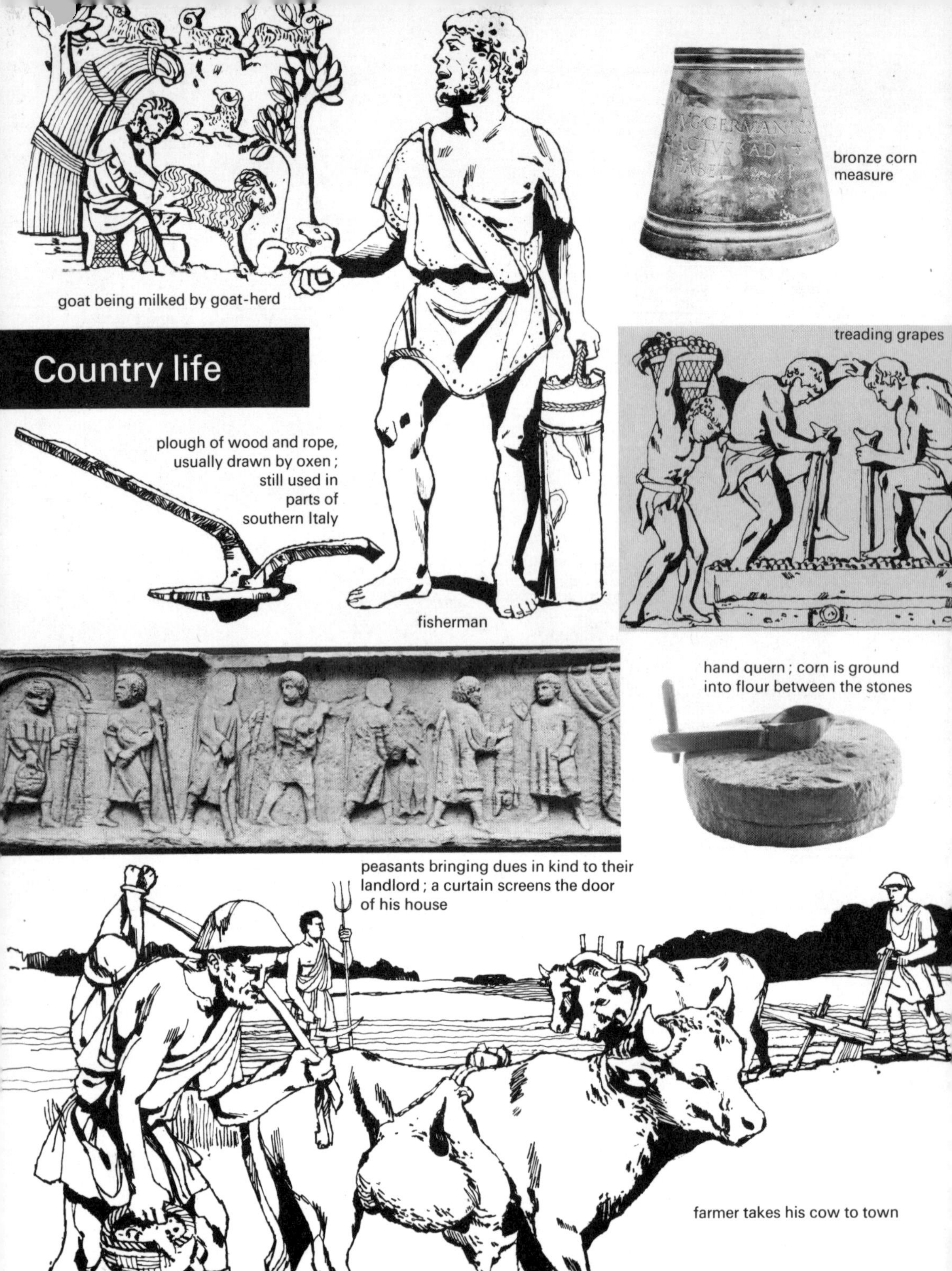

goat being milked by goat-herd

fisherman

bronze corn measure

treading grapes

plough of wood and rope, usually drawn by oxen; still used in parts of southern Italy

hand quern; corn is ground into flour between the stones

peasants bringing dues in kind to their landlord; a curtain screens the door of his house

farmer takes his cow to town

During the time of the emperors Rome depended largely on her army, but farming was always the most important occupation. And throughout Roman times vines supplied grapes for eating and for making into wine, and olive groves the oil which was used for food and cooking, for washing purposes and as fuel for lamps. Country villas with their surrounding estates were attractive places in which to live, and many writers

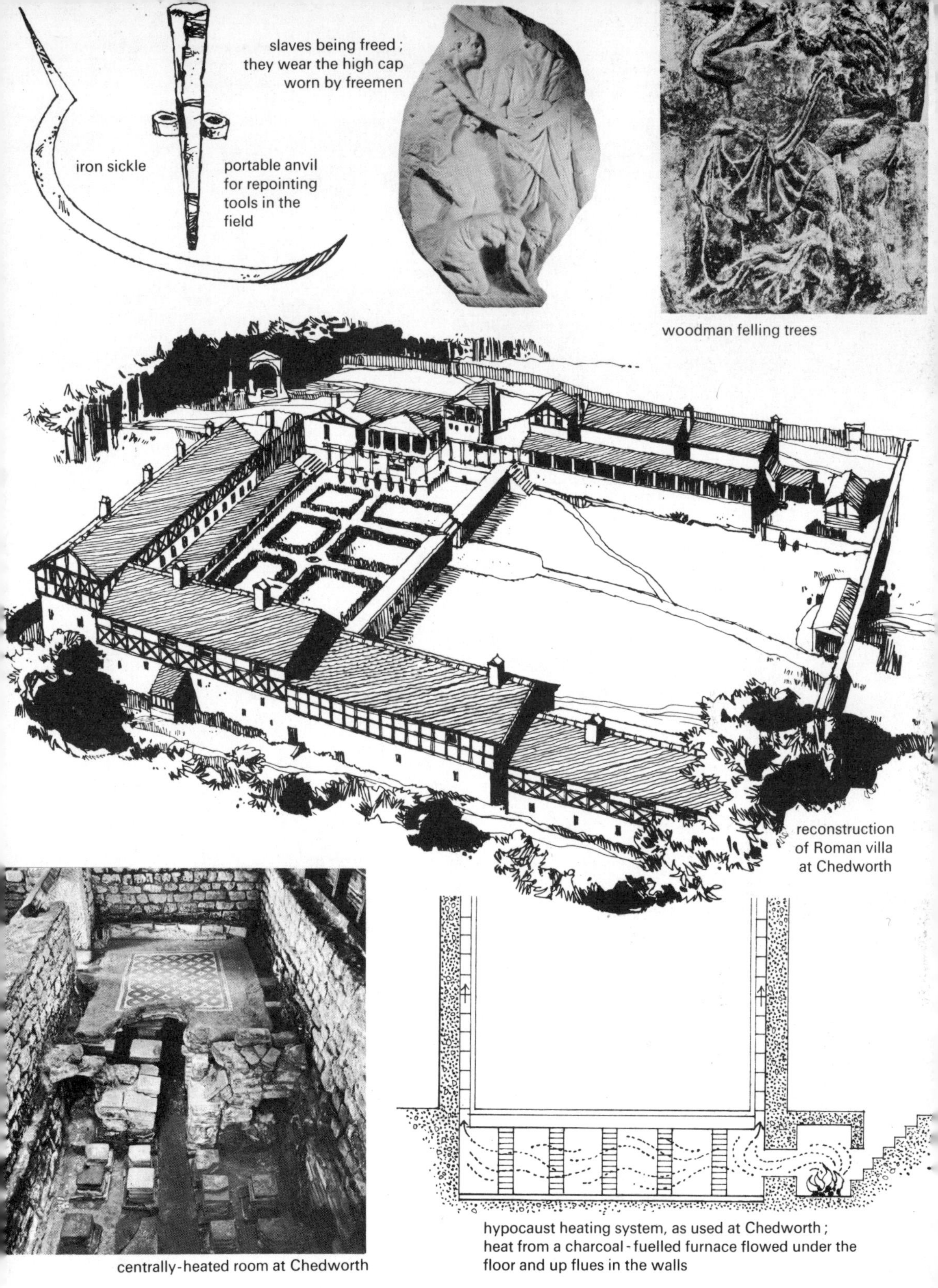

extolled the virtues of country living. From Cato and from the poet Virgil we have descriptions of how the farmer went about his work. Sheep-rearing was always important. When the importing of wheat made the growing of corn less profitable, landowners turned to cattle-breeding. Market gardens flourished around Rome, and supplied green vegetables and root-crops, as well as flowers, which were much in demand at festival times.

The emperor Hadrian, during whose reign, in about AD 120, the Romans built the 70 mile wall from the Tyne to the Solway

THE ROMAN EMPIRE

The shaded area shows the extent of the Roman Empire in AD 67, during the reign of the emperor Nero

indicates where Roman legions were stationed at that time

---- the route of Hannibal's march in 218 BC

Roman provinces are indicated in bold capitals

Numbers in circles refer to significant battles in Roman history (see key on page 17)

Plan of the Battle of Bibracte 58 BC, at which Caesar defeated the Helvetii in his first great battle in Gaul

Caesar drew up his four legions in three lines (**R**). The Helvetii, in close packed columns, advanced and attacked (**H**), but were thrown into confusion by the Roman javelins. Then Caesar advanced. The Helvetii retired to a hill to the north (**H2**). Caesar wheeled to face them, but was attacked at the rear by a force of Boii and Tulingi, who had then arrived (**B – T**). The third Roman line turned about (**R2**), while the first two (**R3**) faced the Helvetii once more, who returned to the attack (**H3**). Both enemy forces were defeated and the Helvetii fled.

Cleopatra (69 – 30 BC)
Queen of Egypt

KEY TO BATTLES

1 **Veseris** 340 BC Romans subdue Latins
2 **Caudine Forks** 321 BC Samnites trap and defeat a whole Roman army
3 **Sentinum** 295 BC Final victory over Samnites
4 **Beneventum** 275 BC Defeat of Pyrrhus, King of Epirus
5 **Mylae** 260 BC First Roman naval victory, over Carthage
6 **Aegates** 241 BC Further naval victory. Carthage makes peace
7 **Telamon** 225 BC Great defeat of Gauls
8 **Lake Trasimene** 217 BC Hannibal defeats Romans
9 **Cannae** 216 BC Further victory by Hannibal
10 **Zama** 202 BC Defeat of Hannibal. End of Second Punic War
11 **Cynoscephalae** 197 BC Defeat of Philip of Macedon
12 **Magnesia** 190 BC Defeat of Antiochus of Syria
13 146 BC Romans destroy Carthage
14 133 BC Fall of Numantia
15 **Vercellae** 101 BC Defeat of Cimbri
16 **Orchomenus** 85 BC Defeat of Mithradates of Pontus
17 **Rhegium** 71 BC End of slave revolt under Spartacus
18 **Bibracte** 58 BC Caesar defeats Helvetii
19 **Carrhae** 53 BC Parthians defeat Rome
20 **Alesia** 52 BC Defeat of Vercingetorix and end of Gaulish revolt
21 **Pharsalus** 48 BC Caesar defeats Pompey
22 **Zela** 47 BC Caesar defeats Pharnaces, son of Mithradates
23 **Thapsus** 46 BC Caesar crushes supporters of Pompey
24 **Munda** 45 BC Final defeat of Pompeians
25 **Philippi** 42 BC Caesar defeats Brutus and Cassius
26 **Actium** 31 BC Roman fleet defeats Antony and Cleopatra
27 **Saltus Teutoburgiensis** 9 Arminius destroys Roman army
28 **Camulodunum** 43 Romans defeat Caractacus
29 61 Romans defeat Iceni under Boudicca
30 **Lugdunum** 197 Severus defeats Albinus, who had proclaimed himself Emperor
31 **Adrianople** 378 Defeat of eastern Emperor Valeus by Goths
32 **Chalons** 451 Defeat of Attila the Hun

Hercules on composite capital from Baths of Caracalla

Rome

Baths of Caracalla; public baths constructed by Emperor Caracalla in 3rd century AD
drawing by Richard Leacroft from *The buildings of Ancient Rome*

1 Temple of Vesta
2 Regia
3 Rostra (speakers' platform)
4 Curia (senate house)
5 Temple of Julius Caesar
6 Temple of Castor and Pollux
7 Basilica Julia
8 Capitol
9 Temple of Juno Moneta
10 Temple of Jupiter Capitolinus
11 Forum Romanum

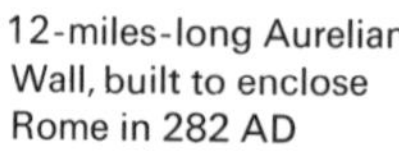

12-miles-long Aurelian Wall, built to enclose Rome in 282 AD

Temple of Portunu

The sixth century BC saw the real beginnings of the city of Rome. A few small villages were united and a $5\frac{1}{2}$ mile defensive wall, known as the Servian wall after King Servius Tullius, was built round them.

This wall enclosed the seven hills in the area. About 600 years later, when London was probably no more than a tiny village at a crossing point of the Thames, Rome had grown to a packed, noisy city of a million inhabitants.

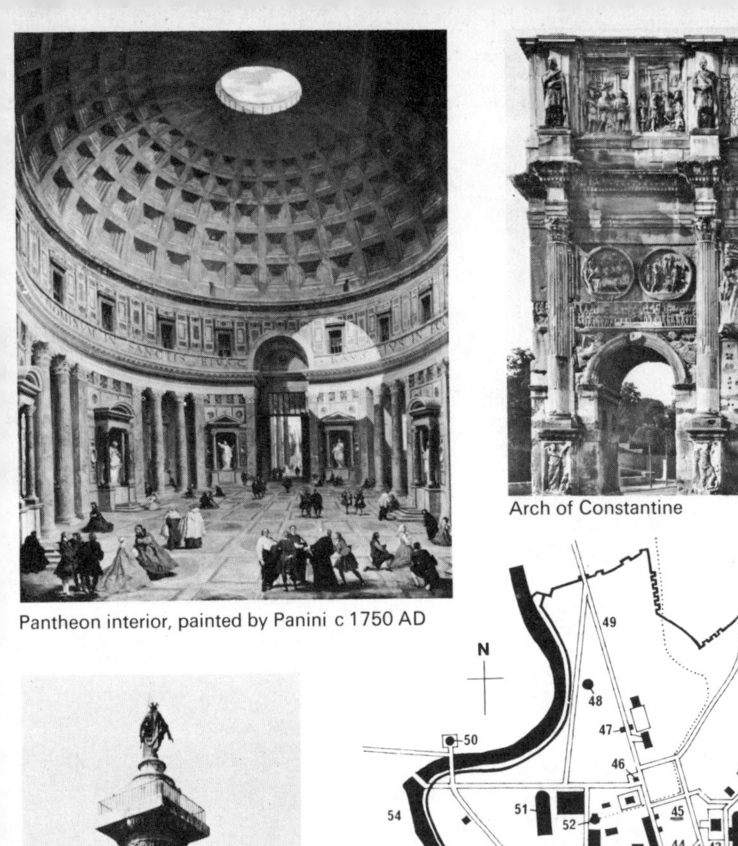

Pantheon interior, painted by Panini c 1750 AD

Arch of Constantine

marble column of Marcus Aurelius; reliefs portray battles in the Marcomannic War

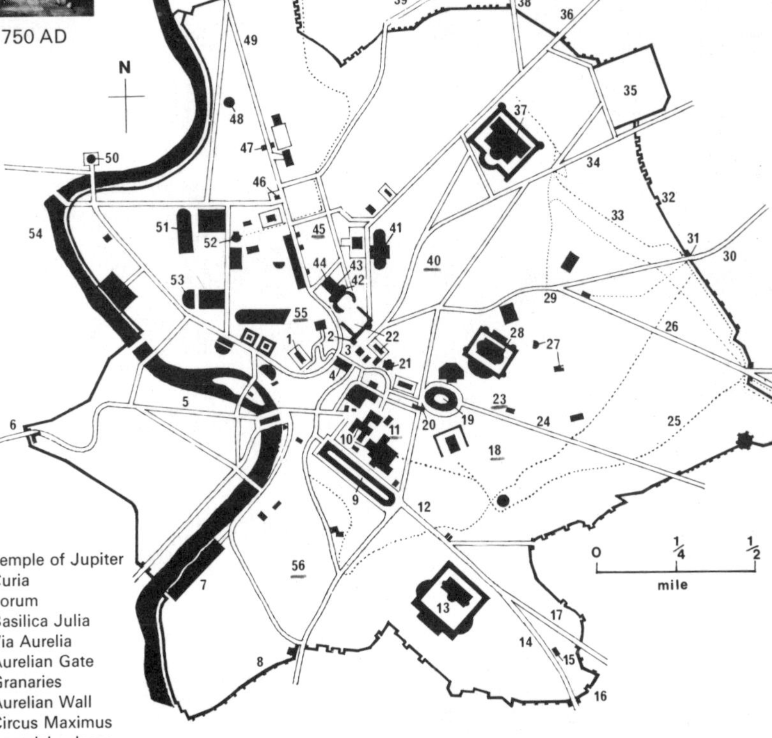

1 Temple of Jupiter
2 Curia
3 Forum
4 Basilica Julia
5 Via Aurelia
6 Aurelian Gate
7 Granaries
8 Aurelian Wall
9 Circus Maximus
10 Imperial palaces
11 Palatine Hill
12 Via Appia
13 Baths of Caracalla
14 Via Appia
15 Tomb of the Scipios
16 Appian Gate
17 Via Latina
18 Caelian Hill
19 Colosseum
20 Arch of Constantine
21 Basilica of Constantine
22 Imperial fora
23 Esquiline Hill
24 Via Tusculana
25 Aqua Claudia
26 Via Labicana
27 Domus Aurea
28 Baths of Trajan
29 Esquiline Gate
30 Via Tiburtina
31 Tiburtine Gate
32 Aurelian Wall
33 Aqua Marcia
34 Via Tiburtina Vetus
35 Praetorian Camp
36 Via Nomentana
37 Baths of Diocletian
38 Via Salaria
39 Via Pinciana
40 Viminal Hill
41 Baths of Constantine
42 Forum of Trajan
43 Trajan's Column
44 Temple of Trajan
45 Quirinal Hill
46 Column of Marcus Aurelius
47 Ara Pacis
48 Mausoleum of Augustus
49 Via Flaminia
50 Tomb of Hadrian
51 Stadium of Domitian
52 Pantheon
53 Theatre of Pompey
54 River Tiber
55 Capitol
56 Aventine Hill

Its buildings were the wonder of the world, and new aqueducts, bridges, temples, theatres, baths and palaces were always being built. At this time Rome had a police force and a fire-brigade, whose efforts were constantly needed because of the fire hazards in narrow streets and crowded conditions. Several times over the centuries large areas of Rome had to be rebuilt because of fire, notably that of 64 AD, during the reign of Nero.

Architecture

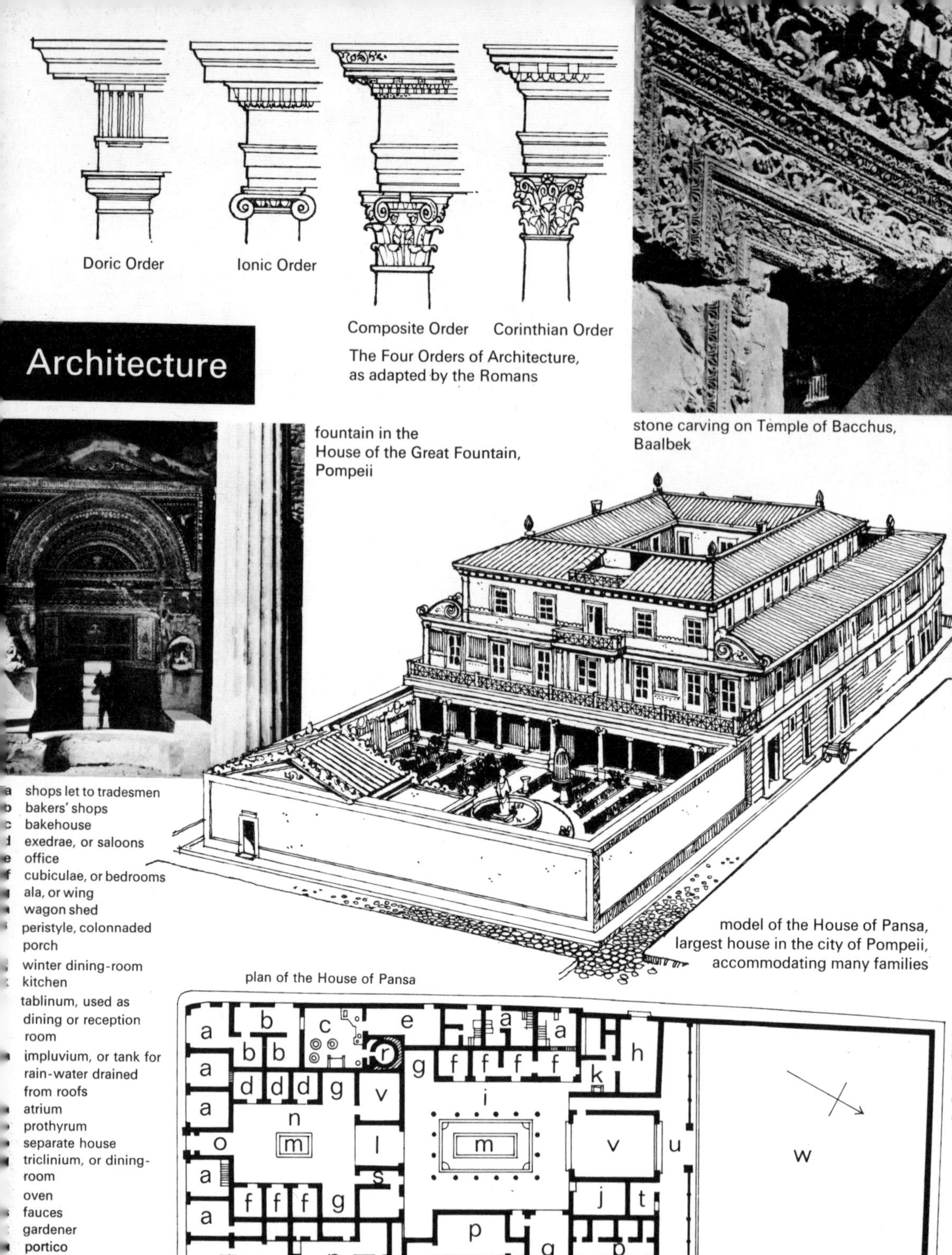

Doric Order

Ionic Order

Composite Order

Corinthian Order

The Four Orders of Architecture, as adapted by the Romans

stone carving on Temple of Bacchus, Baalbek

fountain in the House of the Great Fountain, Pompeii

model of the House of Pansa, largest house in the city of Pompeii, accommodating many families

plan of the House of Pansa

a shops let to tradesmen
b bakers' shops
c bakehouse
d exedrae, or saloons
e office
f cubiculae, or bedrooms
ala, or wing
wagon shed
peristyle, colonnaded porch
winter dining-room
kitchen
tablinum, used as dining or reception room
impluvium, or tank for rain-water drained from roofs
atrium
prothyrum
separate house
triclinium, or dining-room
oven
fauces
gardener
portico
oecus, or reception room
xystus, or garden

The Romans took from the Etruscans the basic shape of their temples. Later they adapted to their own elaborate tastes the architecture of the Greeks, particularly the forms of columns. It was probably the Etruscans who first made good use of the arch, constructed of wedge-shaped stones cunningly put together. But it was the Romans who fully appreciated its possibilities, and employed it in many marvellous ways. By using concrete

street in Pompeii

crane with treadmill worked by human labour

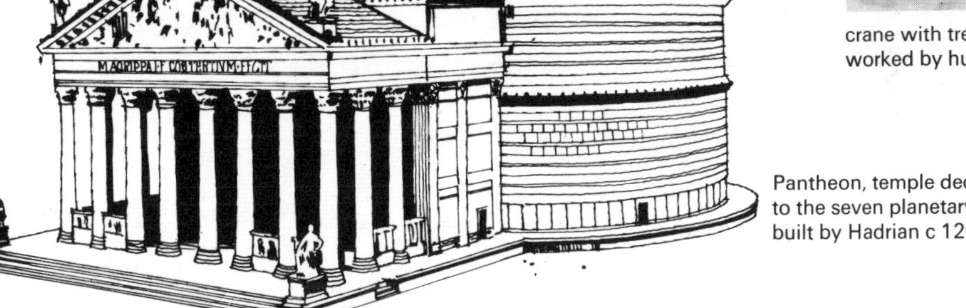

Pantheon, temple dedicated to the seven planetary deities; built by Hadrian c 126 AD

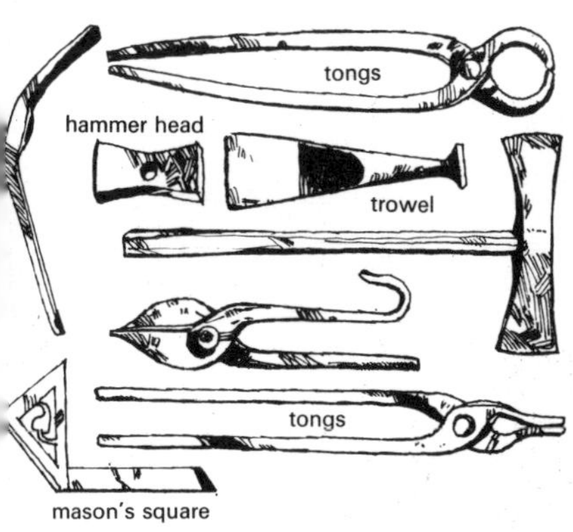

tools used in building

model of Palace of Diocletian, Spalato

they were able to build vast circular buildings with domed roofs, of which the greatest, the Pantheon in Rome, survives more or less intact. This temple had an opening at the top through which light could come.

The Romans liked order, and built many structures of regular brick-work. Bricks were also used in making central heating systems for houses, in which hot air was circulated under the floors and inside the walls.

lamps

family meal

Home and family

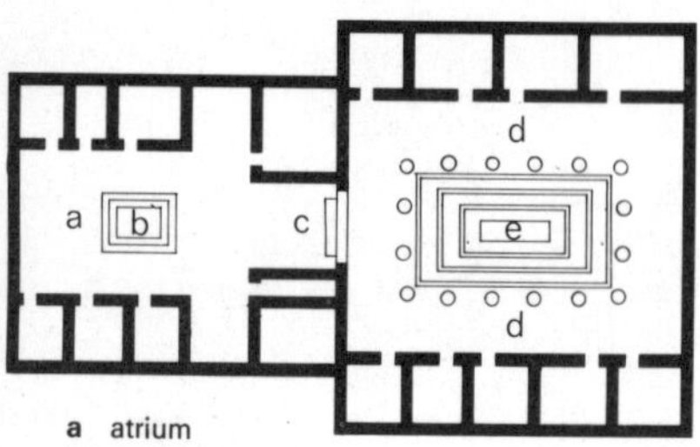

a atrium
b impluvium
c tablinum
d garden court
e fountain

plan of typical house

Roman school in Gaul ; one pupil apologises for arriving late

banquet

The father of the family had complete power over his wife, children, slaves and a number of other people who were not relations but who depended on the family for help. Each household had its own gods, the *lares* and *penates,* as well as the *manes,* the spirits of past ancestors. In early times the main food was a kind of porridge, eaten with green vegetables, which continued to be the staple diet of the poorer classes. Later the

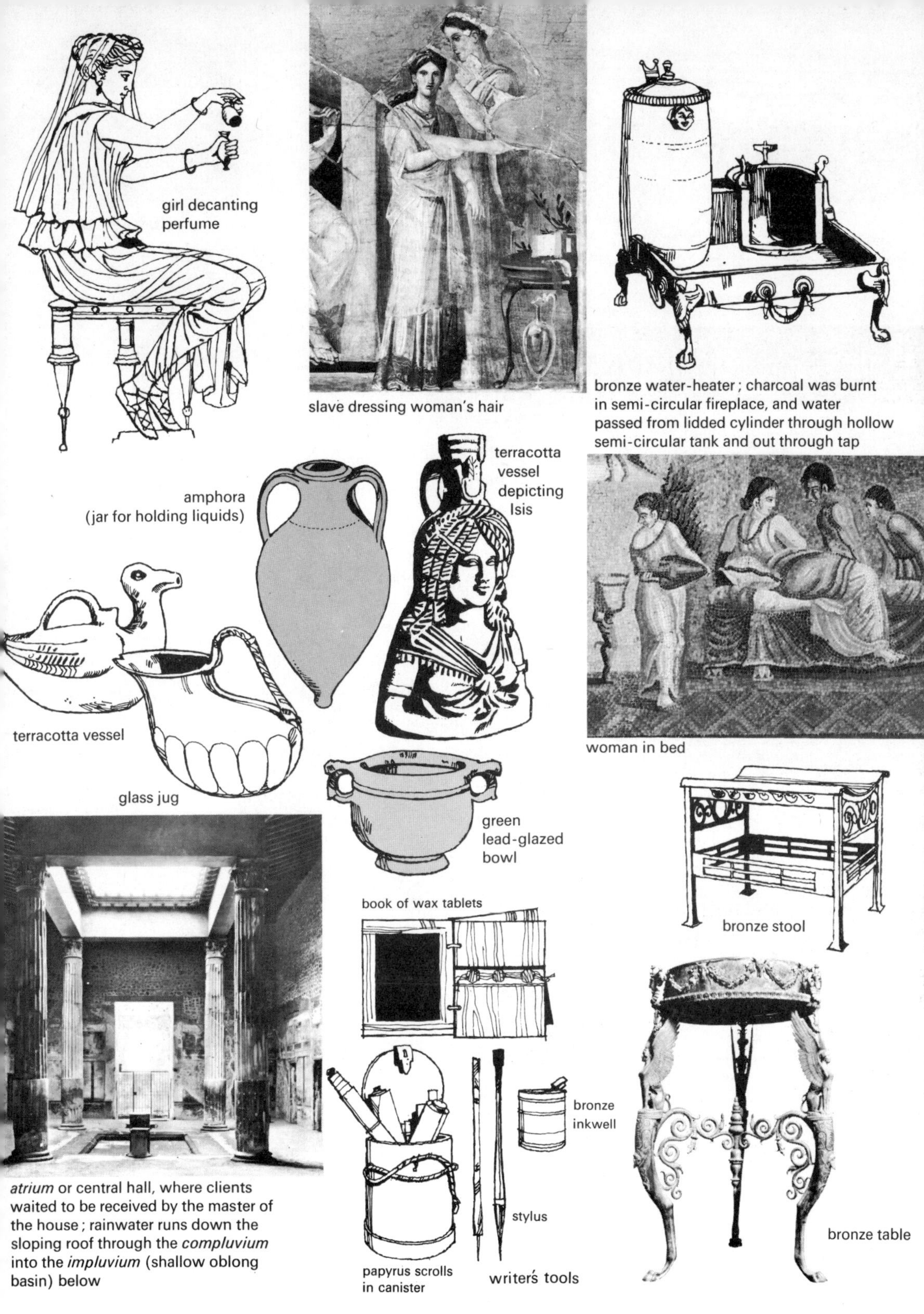

atrium or central hall, where clients waited to be received by the master of the house; rainwater runs down the sloping roof through the *compluvium* into the *impluvium* (shallow oblong basin) below

richer families would have lunch in the middle of the day and a big dinner in the evening, which might be an *hors d'oeuvre* of salad and fish, then meat or chicken and vegetables, followed by fruit. There were no knives or forks, and people ate formal meals lying on couches. Some families also had breakfast, which must have been especially sustaining to the children, who worked hard at school, with no long holidays.

Gods and religion

rites of Dionysus

Mars, god of war

gilt silver bowl showing goddess Roma

high priest of Cybele with ritual symbols and vestments

statue of Jupiter, supreme Roman god

reconstructed Altar of Augustan Peace, Rome

part of certificate of pagan sacrifice, required of all citizens during persecution of Christians

Pan making music

Saturn

Lar, god of the house

The Romans believed that their lives were guided by fate, and that they should look for signs, often by examining the entrails of sacrificed animals, to guide them. Alongside this belief, and the worship of the gods in the home, was the conviction that the well-being of the state depended on the observance of the traditional rites in the public temples. This traditional state religion was bound to Rome and to Roman citizens. There were

dancing faun

Mithras, god of light, killing the bull

she-wolf suckling Romulus and Remus

open incense burner

animals going to sacrifice, led by sacrificing official who brings fruit and incense

man holding death-masks of his ancestors

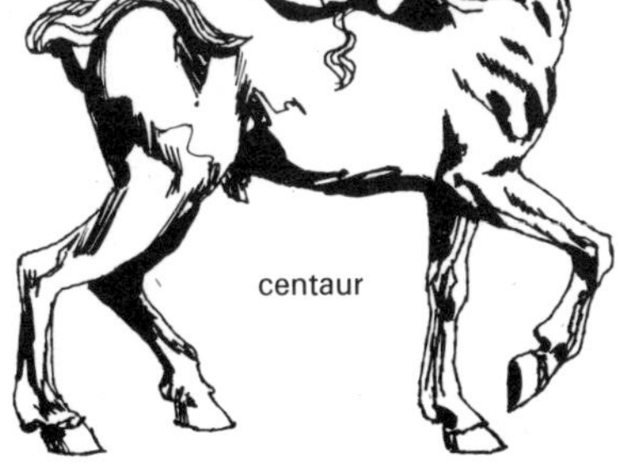

centaur

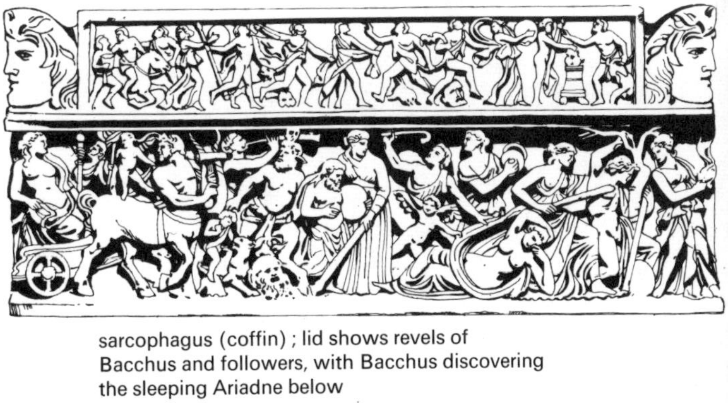

sarcophagus (coffin); lid shows revels of Bacchus and followers, with Bacchus discovering the sleeping Ariadne below

other forms of worship which could be celebrated by all inhabitants of the empire, and Julius Caesar and Augustus were made gods after their deaths; from Egypt came the cult of the mother-goddess Isis; from Persia the worship of Mithras, lord of Light, a favourite of soldiers. But in spite of persecution, followers of Christ succeeded in the end in establishing Christianity in the Roman empire.

Early Christianity

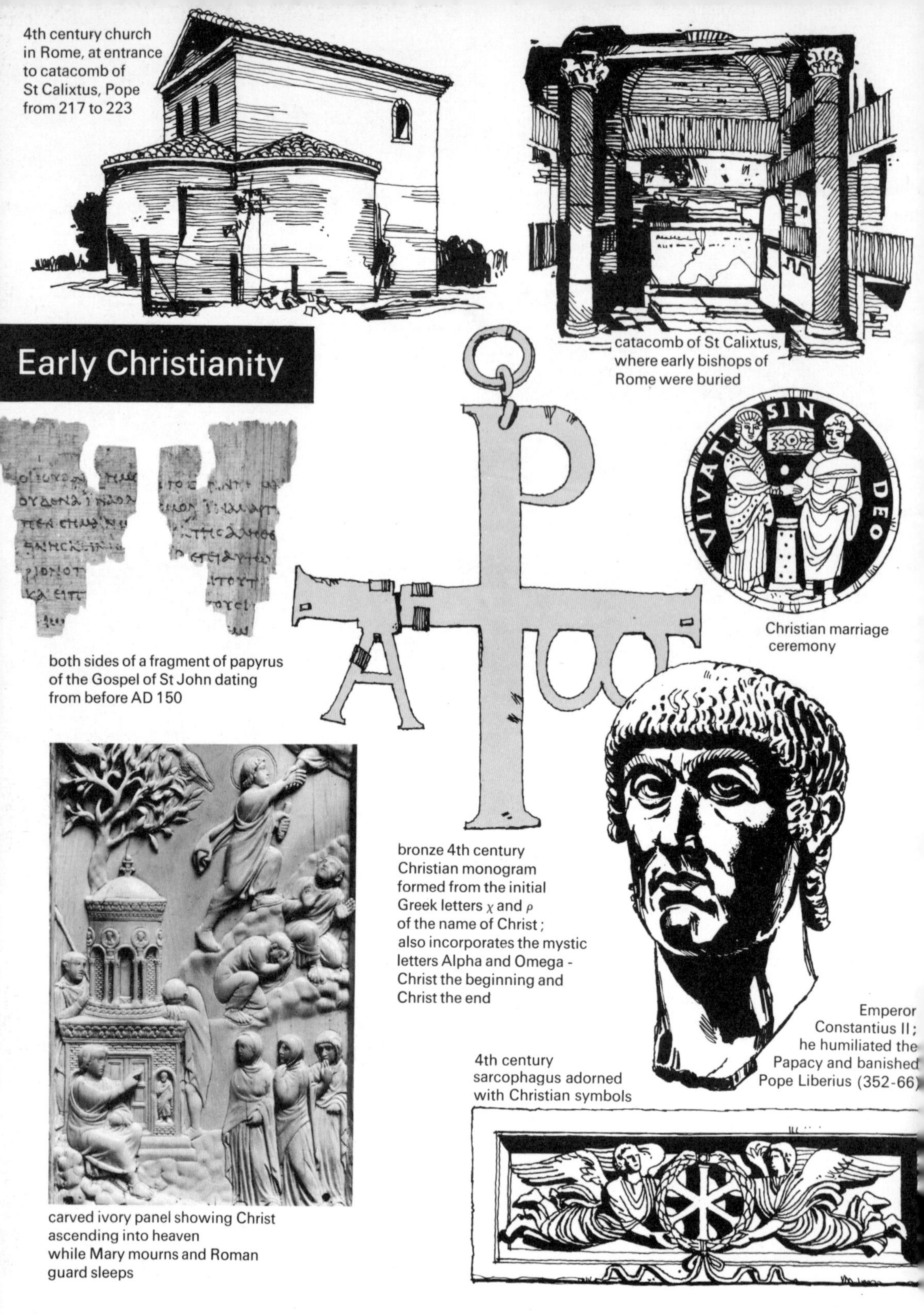

4th century church in Rome, at entrance to catacomb of St Calixtus, Pope from 217 to 223

catacomb of St Calixtus, where early bishops of Rome were buried

Christian marriage ceremony

both sides of a fragment of papyrus of the Gospel of St John dating from before AD 150

bronze 4th century Christian monogram formed from the initial Greek letters χ and ρ of the name of Christ; also incorporates the mystic letters Alpha and Omega - Christ the beginning and Christ the end

carved ivory panel showing Christ ascending into heaven while Mary mourns and Roman guard sleeps

Emperor Constantius II; he humiliated the Papacy and banished Pope Liberius (352-66)

4th century sarcophagus adorned with Christian symbols

To the Romans Christianity meant giving up so many of their old ways and traditions, that they were slow to accept it. But after the dramatic conversion of the emperor Constantine in AD 312, it became the majority religion of the empire. Though the pagan rites and festivals were then abandoned, it was some years still before the gladiatorial combats were stopped, they were so popular.

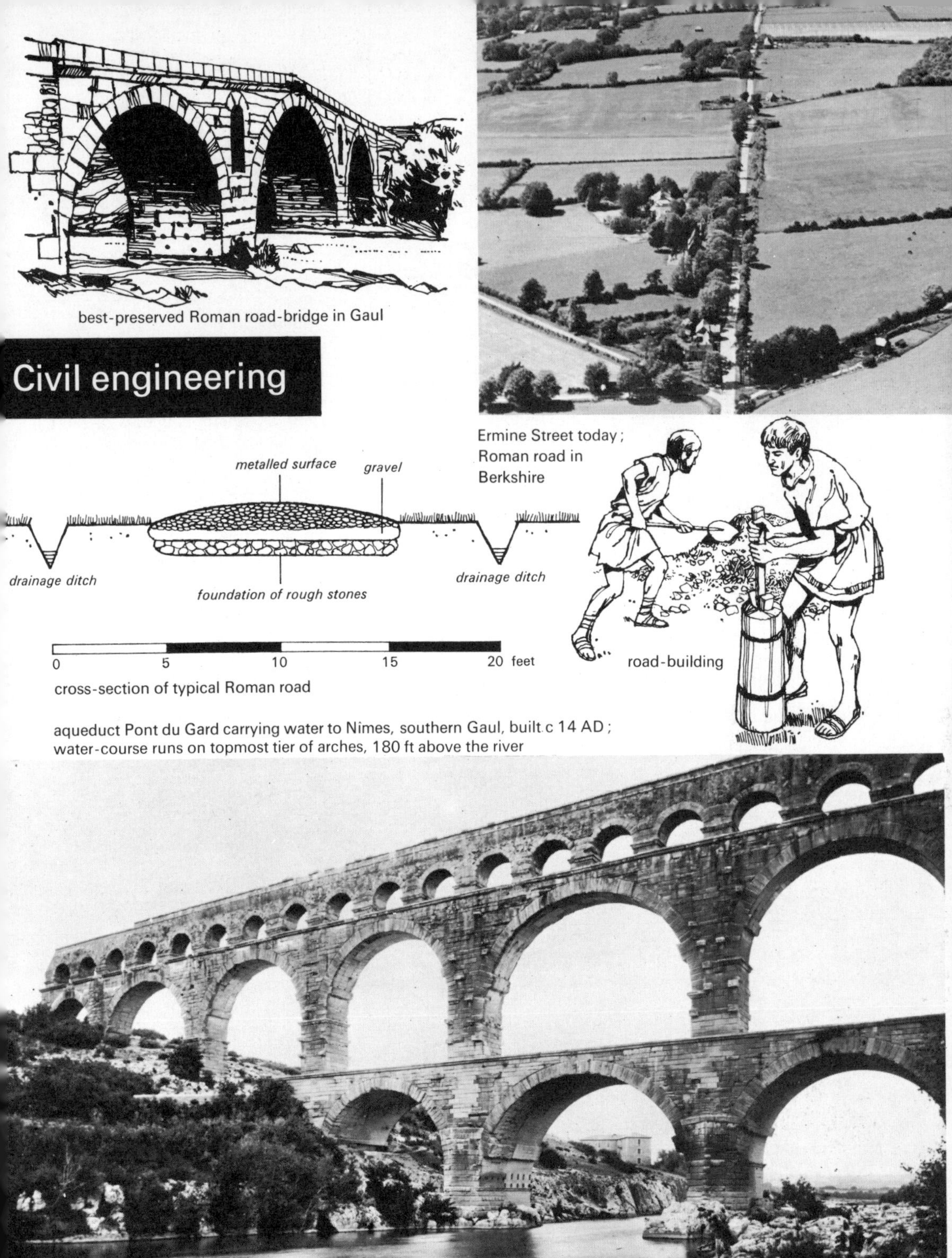

best-preserved Roman road-bridge in Gaul

Civil engineering

Ermine Street today; Roman road in Berkshire

road-building

cross-section of typical Roman road

aqueduct Pont du Gard carrying water to Nimes, southern Gaul, built c 14 AD; water-course runs on topmost tier of arches, 180 ft above the river

For their armies to move quickly to trouble spots throughout the empire, the Romans needed good, straight roads along which to march their forces. Main roads were made by the state, and at each Roman mile a milestone was set. The state also maintained the water supplies, bringing piped water from the mountains to the cities, constructing tall aqueducts to carry the water over valleys and vast plains.

merchant ships

Ships and travel

wine-ship on the Moselle

anchor, with shank and arms of wood and stock of lead

warship with 'castle', gun platform for artillery; carved crocodile is symbol of Libya

warships

Merchant ships sailed between the main ports of the Mediterranean, and other vessels would follow the coast-lines, so that a traveller could easily find a ship to carry him. Storms and pirates were particular hazards, and in 67 BC Pompey attacked the pirates and made sea travel safer. In Rome wheeled vehicles were not allowed during the day, because there would be too much traffic. So wealthy people travelled in litters carried by

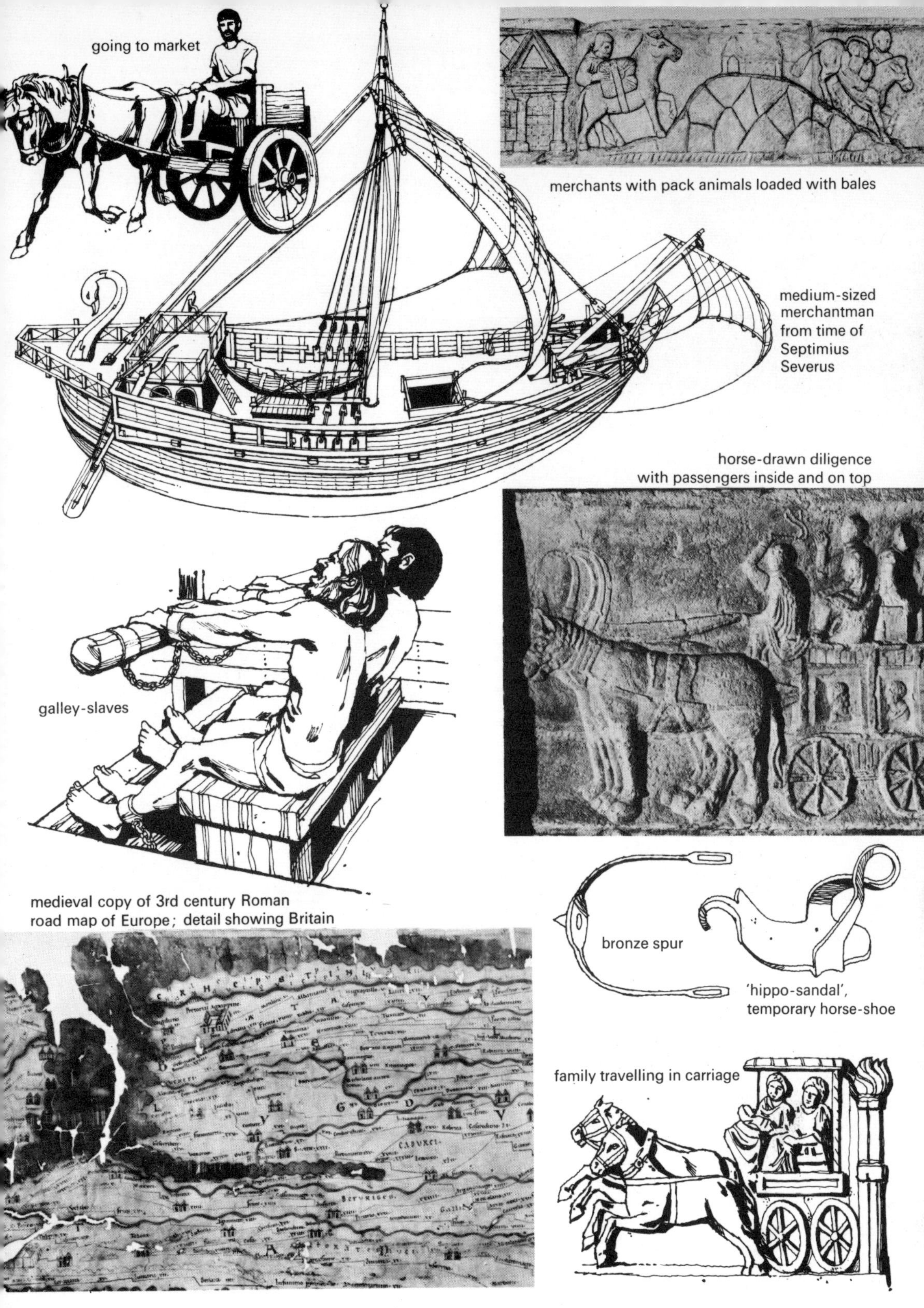

going to market

merchants with pack animals loaded with bales

medium-sized merchantman from time of Septimius Severus

horse-drawn diligence with passengers inside and on top

galley-slaves

medieval copy of 3rd century Roman road map of Europe; detail showing Britain

bronze spur

'hippo-sandal', temporary horse-shoe

family travelling in carriage

slaves. Outside Rome people went in carriages or on horseback, though at this time the stirrup was not known. The poor travelled on foot. There were inns along the way where travellers could spend the night. Augustus established a series of police posts to keep order on the roads, and also started an official postal service, with horses picked up at stages along the route to pull the messenger's carriage.

fasces ; bundles of rods, sometimes with an axe, borne before a magistrate of high grade

Two **CONSULS**—elected annually for one year by the people as a whole through the assembly (in time of emergency Rome could be ruled by a single Dictator, holding office for six months).

THE SENATE—the Governing Body of Rome, which discussed legislation before it was submitted to the people's decision. It also handled foreign affairs and finance. About 600 members, ultimately all of whom had served as government officials.

POPULAR ASSEMBLY—the people met in various assemblies to elect officials and to accept or reject proposed law.

Roman government

in the days of the Republic 509-27 BC

Government officials

PRAETOR (8 during later Republic) *Judge*
Praetors and ex-praetors, like ex-consuls, were most likely to become governors of provinces

CENSOR (2)
Chief registrar, supervisor of morals and leading financial officer

TRIBUNE OF THE PEOPLE *Tribunus plebis* (10)
To protect the rights of the people

AEDILE (4)
Supervisor of the peace and of public works

QUAESTOR
(20 during later Republic)
Financial officer
Minimum age 25, after military service
After 70 BC quaestors automatically became members of the Senate

Cato the Elder
234-149 BC
Roman statesman and writer

Cicero 106-43 BC
Roman orator, philosopher and politician

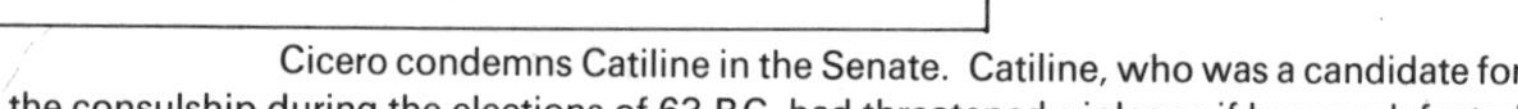

Cicero condemns Catiline in the Senate. Catiline, who was a candidate for the consulship during the elections of 63 BC, had threatened violence if he was defeated.

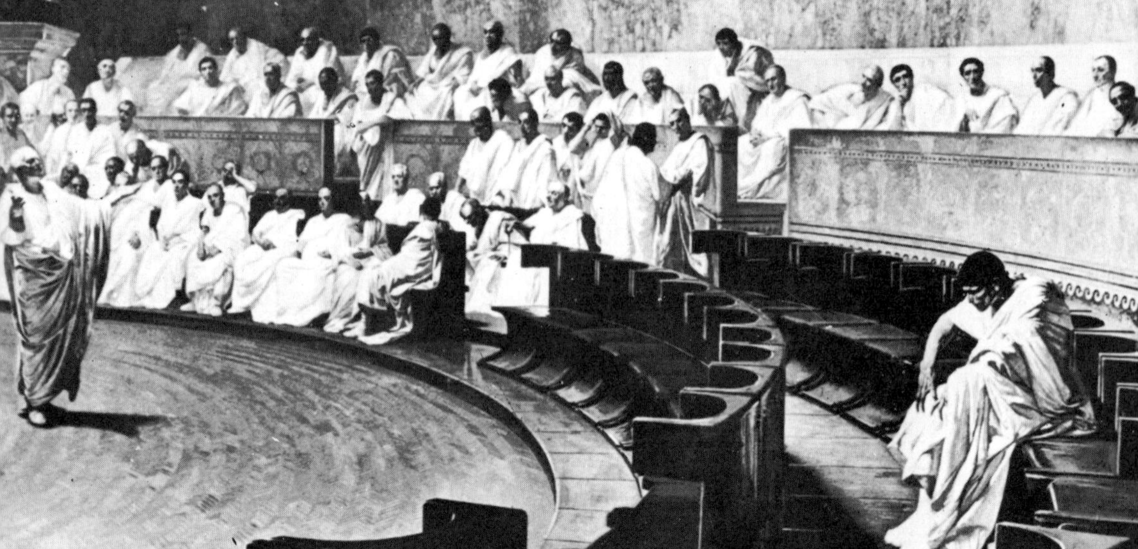

detail from 6th century ivory showing the triumph of an emperor

Byzantine carved capital, Ravenna

The Byzantine Empire

1849 lithograph showing Great Church of St Sophia, Constantinople; dedicated by Justinian in 537

Emperor Justinian and his court

Empress Theodora, wife of Justinian

jewelled cross presented by Emperor Justin II to the Vatican around 575; contains a splinter the Byzantines believed came from the Cross of Christ

silver dish showing Emperor Theodosius I enthroned

Madonna and Child; after a mosaic at Ravenna

The emperor Constantine made Christianity the Roman religion. He established a new capital at Byzantium, which he renamed Constantinople. The Byzantine civilization flourished for centuries, long after the Roman empire was in 395 AD divided into an eastern and a western part. In 410 AD Rome was sacked by the Goths. When Romulus Augustulus, the last Roman Emperor, was deposed in 476 AD, the Roman Empire in the west came to an end.

Administration of a far-flung empire linked to a central government

Communication throughout empire by means of a network of roads

Awareness of importance of systematic measurement, eg use of milestones

Public postal system

Banking system

The legacy of Rome

The family as an important social unit

Roman Law—the idea of impartial justice and verdict by jury

Sanitation, drainage and sewers

Public hospitals

Roman numerals

Modern alphabet

Modern calendar and names of months

Latin literature

Latin language—basis of Italian, Spanish and Portuguese, and French; and of one-third of English language

Use of brick and concrete

Central heating system

Glass windows

Construction of blocks of flats

Use of the arch, eg for bridges, vaulting, domes

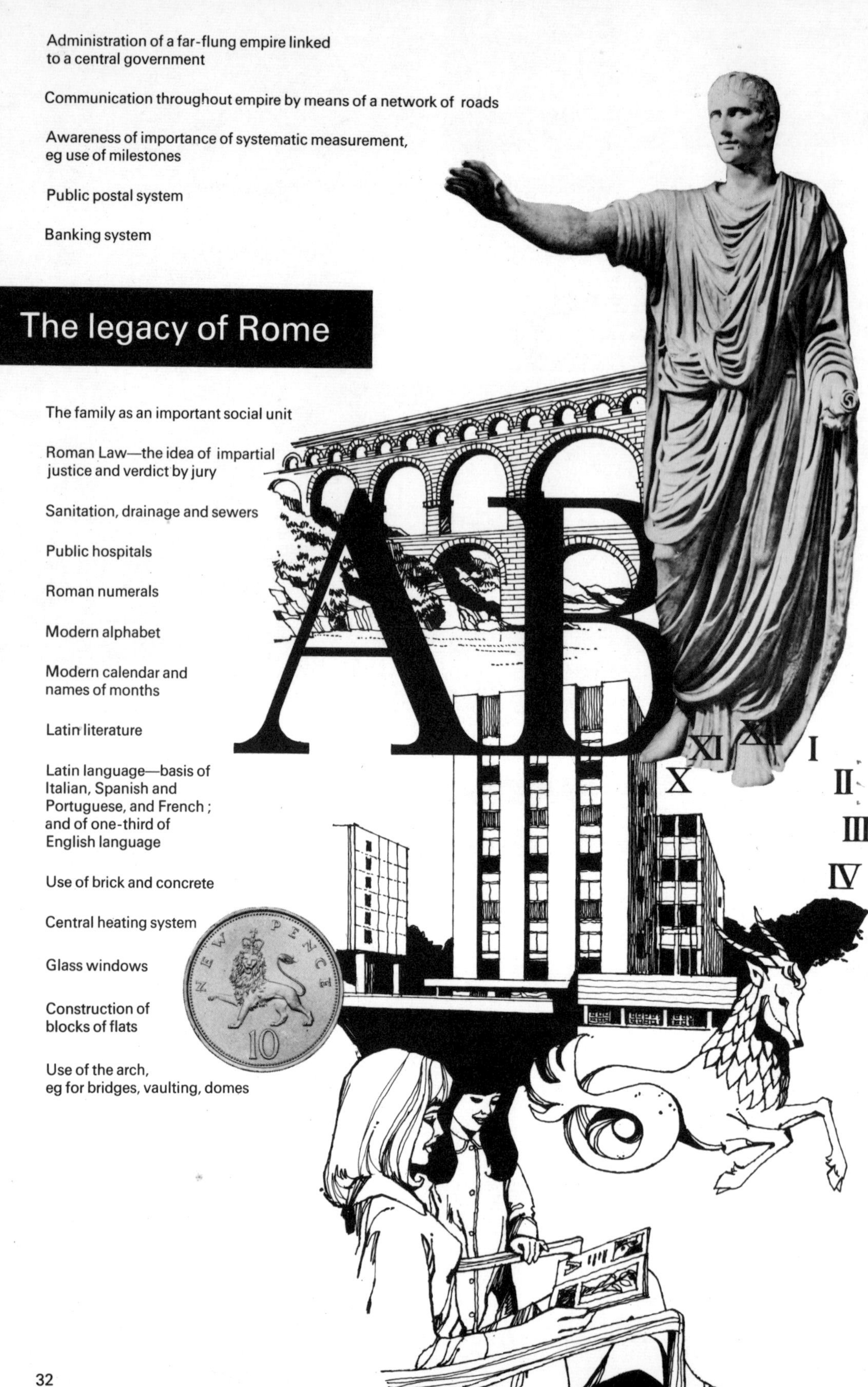